Unspoken Words

sarai pearson

Unspoken Words © 2022 sarai pearson

All rights reserved.

No part of this publication may be reproduced, stored in a retrieval system, or transmitted, in any form or by any means, electronic, mechanical, photocopying, recording or otherwise, without the prior written permission of the presenters.

sarai pearson asserts the moral right to be identified as author of this work.

Presentation by *BookLeaf Publishing*

Web: www.bookleafpub.com

E-mail: info@bookleafpub.com

ISBN: 9789395756815

First edition 2022

Ecstasy

"What's the most painful thing you
experienced?"

love.

"But why? love is beautiful"

Yes, but you see…
everything is temporary;
the pain,
the euphoria,
everything.

Love is Ecstasy;

rush of serotonin,

elation.

but you see…

everything comes to an end;

you can enjoy the ride,

you can take in the feeling,

but eventually...

it will come to an end.

Almost, Always, Never

Almost.
Just before the flowers bloomed-
Winter struck.
Vibrant shades of yellow, pink, and purple,
Covered with the clouds of grey.
Something so close, to being so beautiful,
But not quite.
Almost.

Always.
A promise between two souls,
A contract held with no conditions-
Signed with the ink of love,
To hold the umbrella
When the rain begins to pour,
Always.

Never.
Heartbreak of all.
Almost is not always,
It is not promised nor certain,
Almost is never enough.
The hands of possibility,
Gripping to reality-
Slip right through.

Almost,
But… never enough
Never.

Guns and Poems

Take your finger off the trigger,
take away the gun,
fill your hand with pen and ink,
and write your pain and sorrows
through the words of a poem.
Let the tone be your bullet,
as it fills the room
with a beautiful melody,
striking the page,
with the hopes of tomorrow…

Miss Universe

She wasn't like the rest;
she never wanted the spotlight,
she spoke softly,
never wanting the attention…
but all eyes
went to her.
Not just a star,
but her own planet.
Her own gravitational pull
attracts more than just the eye;
She attracts the mind,
the body,
the soul.
Miss Universe,
they called her.

Blue

Blue.
The color of sadness,
the color that brings one down
Associate with negativity;
from stormy nights-
to lonely days
The color of sadness.

Yet all i see is blue
when i look at you;
I see the tides hitting shore,
the beautiful clear sky,
the rain after a drought-
there is no doubt
that you,
give blue,
a new meaning.

The Realization

The world keeps spinning,
Yet I don't know why.
The body that I'm in
doesn't feel like mine
I never knew how the world worked,
with so many questions…
with not enough answers.

Until one day I finally knew-
that I am me,
and you are you.
I am more than my body.
I am more than what you see.
A broken soul ready to flee.
Nobody to mend what has been broken,
until I heard the words that's been spoken;
The one who can fix me is me.
It will take some time,
it's a long path,
but deep down I know
the love I'll feel,
is bound to last

Hopeless Romantic

To be a hopeless romantic is silly.
For how something could be so beautiful,
yet hopeless?
Until you fall too fast,
too hard,
landing out of reach,
of one who feels so close…
yet they slip
right from your fingertips.
One step too far.
Too much distance,
and too much space.
Just one wish away,
from fantasy-
to reality,
from hopeless-
to hopeful.

Forever and Always

Everything is temporary,
coming to an end.
Yet time is limitless,
and as every second passes by,
She holds onto the love
a little tighter,
praying the end isn't near.
She loves without condition,
with no limit.
Near or far,
she will love,

Forever and Always

She will love.

Hypocrite

I am a hypocrite-
not in the way they may think,
but in a way where i say "hold on"
knowing my fingers are slipping.
When I say "keep going"
knowing that i had already quit.
I say life is worth living,
but that doesn't include mine
keep smiling,
but I'm crying inside
love life,
but I hate mine
this constant battle is tearing me down,
eating me up,
ruining me.
Yet you're the warrior
and I'm the hypocrite.
I could give you a million reasons
to stay alive
but none for myself,
a million people who love you
but not one who loves me,
it's kinda funny cause-
I'm the happy friend;

the one who's always laughing,
who gives great advice-
advice I never take
I guess I'm a hypocrite in many ways.
And as you hear me speak
of my pain and troubles
I don't wish for your pity,
instead, I ask of one thing;
don't be like me,
don't be a hypocrite,
don't hide your pain,
don't shy away,
remember it's okay to not be okay
and please
check on your friends
they may be hypocrites too.

Simple Solution

It's funny how everything can be fixed,
with the most simple solution.
A band aid to cover the wound,
to allow it to heal,
allow it be anew again.
A crack in the sidewalk sealed with cement,
covering the damage, the imperfections
Anew again.

When you walked out of my life…my heart
shattered into a million pieces,
a million pieces that can be fixed,
with a band aid, right?
Because after all…
everything can be fixed,
with the most simple solution.

So simple that I was blinded.
Right in my face, yet my vision is blurry.
For how could I not know,
that my simple solution…
would be in the shape of another person.
Someone who loves me with their whole being,
someone who values me for all that I am.
They showed me love in a new light.

For how could I not know,
that I would be…
my simple solution.

Rain

Many preferred the sunshine and clear skies.
They only come when you're your brightest,
they only loved your warmth and best days.
But they don't see the beauty of your clouds,
the delicate shades of white and grey,
hovering over the sky.
They don't see the beauty of your rain.
You nourish my soul as you touch my skin,
you wash away my pain and sorrows,
cleansing my being.
Feeding my roots,
helping my flowers bloom.
How could they not know,
the power of your rain.

My Friend

I'm never truly alone,
I have a friend who lives within me.
Some days she speaks softly to me,
others I am not enough.
She speaks to me in a way in which nobody can
hear,
through thoughts that will fill my head
building my self-esteem,
that quickly gets stripped away.
I never know if my friend truly likes me,
she changes her opinions on me
quite frequently,
quite rapidly.
I try to earn her love,
earn her trust,
I try to nurture her,
care for her
but it is not enough.
I am never truly alone,
but sometimes…
I wish I was

Numerical Value

They say words hold power of the world,
yet what they fail to tell,
is the power of a number.
These numbers hold a power that cannot be
measured by its worth,
for it tells us ours.
From the day we enter this world,
we are held captive by this
from our age,
to our weight,
our worth is measured by the numbers
that tells us how much value we hold.
Yet, just like malicious thief,
life always has a trick up her sleeve,
robbing us of our self-worth
as the numbers go up,
our value goes down.
Quality over quantity
yet when I hold more weight on my body,
more years to my life
my quality lessens
day by day,
life is playing a game
ran by the numbers
and I am bound to lose

War

After years of war,
she finally goes home
accepting defeat.
By the time the door opens
the feeling of excitement that once was
has quickly drained from her body
and fills with regret.
Mother and father,
who use to spend their days smiling,
are now weeping.
Brother and sister,
who use to run around the house,
laughing
are now still in shock,
being too young
unable to process.
She's struck with disbelief,
this was not what she had expected.
But how could they have known…
that she had went to war by herself
within herself,
battling the demons of depression
who had won her life.

Picture Perfect

Picture perfect.
The moment captured in time
displays the joyous smiles,
capturing the love of two souls
gazing into one another,
the right moment in time…
caught on camera
and it is,
picture perfect.

For it is all an illusion.
Behind the camera;
screaming, pain and sorrows
fill the atmosphere.
Love suddenly shifting
to a feeling just as strong,
filling the soul with rage.
Behind the camera;
displays the fade of smiles,
as tears fill the eyes
watery vision,
blurs the scene
of what should be…
picture perfect.

My Star

It's funny how every star
floats in space,
light years away,
but they're always there
with every person,
every night
they answer questions
they lead the way.
I wonder if…
there's any way,
connected to both
they led me to one,
just as bright as them
just as beautiful,
if they had led me….
to you

Sunflower

She stands tall among the rest,
in a crowd,
yet she stands alone.
The softest petals,
gently blows with the breeze
the brightest of yellows
shines even in the darkest of nights.

You couldn't help but stare;
drawn to the flower,
for not just the petals,
but the roots hidden…
deep in the earth
remain unseen
for what does it hold
seeds of secrets
remain untold

For she is more than just her petal.
She is the roots.
The roots hidden in the earth
crying to be seen
the seeds of secrets
bound to unfold
for that is she beyond the petals

for she is the brightest sunflower.

One Day

One day,
one day I will forget your touch;
the way our fingers would interlock,
and the way my hand brushed your cheek.
I'll forget how soft your skin is,
how safe it made me feel
with my head on your chest,
listening to the beat of a heart
that is no longer mine.

One day I will forget your eyes;
the way they sparkled as the sun would set,
and the way they shrunk when you smiled.
I'll forget those nights I got lost,
in the stars of space,
that you hold within your eyes
never wanting to go back.

One day I'll forget your voice;
your words soothing like the tides,
uncontrollable like the waves.
I will always remember the words you spoke to
me;
the way they became who i am,

I am the roots, no longer me
I am the tree of the words.
stuck in the grounds of the earth,
branching out for help,
I am no longer me.
I am you,
I am the tree you grew,
watered with your words,
trimmed into your perfect image.

One day the tree will be cut;
stripping away the identity you once gave me,
no longer me,
no longer you.
The seeds will be replanted,
a new tree will grow,
a new identity,
a new me.
One day…

You

You.
The difference between truth and sincerity,
the space between the lines.
Between love and lust,
heart and mind,
it's you.
The genuine feelings,
the raw emotion,
it's always you.
Three letters,
two souls,
one difference…
intertwined and connected
it's always been you.

Two not One

There is no such thing as one.
As everything comes in a pair,
unable to exist without the other.
We fail to know happiness,
unless we already met sorrow.
The joyous smiles cannot blossom,
unless they have been nurtured by our tears.
We fail to meet love,
without the introduction of heartbreak.
For how can we know we're whole…
if we've never been broken.
We fail to see beauty,
unless we feel the pain
as it lingers inside the false perception,
of what we see as beauty and grace
One does not exist,
it all begins with two
without the other…
it is unknown, unheard, and unfelt

We as people, feel as if we're whole,
but one does not exist,
In order to reach true certainty,
we must find our second heart,
to complete the one we carry.

two brings balance into our twisted world
it proves the existence
of what was once…
the unknown, the unheard, the unfelt

Natural

We wish upon the naturals
with the desire to bring our dreams
to reality.
We wish upon the naturals,
as they fill our hearts with hope,
and fill our souls with joy.
The naturals bring proof to the world,
that the most beautiful things
live around us, surrounding us with grace.

A wish upon a star,
holding onto something that feels
out of reach, out of touch,
gently slipping from the fingertips.
But the naturals remind us
that near or far,
we are surrounded by beauty,
surrounded by grace.
Just like the stars that fill the empty night sky,
with the bright lights of hope.
For that's why I wish upon the naturals.

A wish upon a dandelion,
whole, it is our dreams.
When blowing on our dreams,

we watch the possibilities fill the air
letting the wind drift, them away
where they touch the Earth's soil,
seeping into the ground…
in order to grow more dreams,
to fill the air with more possibilities,
for that's why we wish upon the naturals.

www.ingramcontent.com/pod-product-compliance
Lightning Source LLC
LaVergne TN
LVHW021354200726

843509LV00014B/2850

9789395756815